Love, Life, and Loss:
A Search for Answers in Grief

Harold G. Birkenhead

Parson's Porch Books

Love, Life, and Loss: A Search for Answers in Grief
ISBN: Softcover 979-8-89532-028-0
Copyright © 2025 by Harold G. Birkenhead

All rights reserved. No part of this book may be reproduced or transmitted in any form or by any means, electronic or mechanical, including photocopying, recording, or by any information storage and retrieval system, without permission in writing from the publisher.

Parson's Porch Books is an imprint of Parson's Porch & Company (PP&C) in Cleveland, Tennessee. PP&C is a self-funded charity which earns money by publishing books of noted authors, representing all genres. Its face and voice is **David Russell Tullock** (dtullock@parsonsporch.com).

Parson's Porch & Company *turns books into bread & milk* by sharing its profits with the poor.

www.parsonsporch.com

Love, Life, and Loss:
A Search for Answers in Grief

Dedication

To Charlene, my beloved wife of 43 years—your love, inspiration, and unwavering guidance shaped the essence of who I am. This book is a tribute to your memory, a celebration of your spirit, and a testament to the profound impact you had on my life, and the lives of so many. You are forever cherished, forever loved. Harry

Contents

Dedication..5
Synopsis of Love, Life, and Loss..............................9
Introduction...11
Prelude..15
   Love, Life, and Loss: A Search for Answers in Grief
Chapter One...21
   Eternal Life—Death Is Not The End
Chapter Two...27
   The Foundation of Love
Chapter Three..33
   Family As Legacy
Chapter Four..39
   The Impact of Friendship and Community and the Rippling Effects of Kindness
Chapter Five...47
   Trials and Tribulations
Chapter Six...53
   Loss and Grief as Teachers
Chapter Seven..61
   Service to Others
Chapter Eight:..67
   Spiritual Reflections
Chapter Nine..71
   Conclusion: Finding the Answer
Chapter Ten..77
   Sixteen Exercises to Help Cope with Grief

"*I have lived with you and loved you, and now you are gone. Gone where I cannot follow, until I have finished all of my days.* – Victoria Hanley

Synopsis of Love, Life, and Loss: A Search for Answers in Grief

Love, Life, and Loss: A Search for Answers in Grief is a heartfelt exploration of how love shapes us, how loss transforms us, and how, through both, we uncover the deeper truths of our existence. Drawing from the author's personal journey through the devastating loss of his wife, Charlene, and their beloved dog, Cooper, this book offers an intimate look at grief's many layers and its potential to awaken profound spiritual growth.

The narrative unfolds in three interconnected parts:

1. Love and Life: The first section celebrates the bonds of love and the shared moments that give life meaning. Through vivid storytelling, the author reflects on his marriage, the joy and challenges of their journey together, and the unique connection with their dog, Cooper. These moments set the stage for understanding how deeply intertwined love and life are with the human experience.

2. Loss and Grief: The second section delves into the raw and often disorienting emotions of loss. It offers readers an unfiltered account of the author's struggles—from the silence that followed Charlene's passing to the compounded grief of losing Cooper shortly after. Through honest reflection, readers gain insight into the universality of grief and its power to connect us all in our humanity.

3. Healing and Transformation: The final section reveals how the author turned to spiritual practices, such as

meditation, contemplation, and dream work, to navigate his grief. Using tools like Hemi-Sync technology, he rediscovered his connection to Charlene and Cooper, not in their physical absence, but in the eternal presence of their love. This transformative journey inspires readers to see loss not as an ending, but as a gateway to deeper self-awareness and spiritual growth.

Blending memoir with practical guidance, *Love, Life, and Loss* is more than a story of personal loss; it is a roadmap for anyone seeking answers in their own grief. The book's central message is one of hope: even in the face of unimaginable pain, we have the capacity to heal, grow, and find meaning in the extraordinary gifts life offers—gifts that often come disguised as loss.

Written with compassion and authenticity, this book is a companion for anyone navigating grief, an inspiration for spiritual seekers, and a reminder that love endures, always.

Introduction

I drove aimlessly through familiar streets as Jelly Roll's song, *"I'm Not Okay, But It's All Gonna Be Alright,"* played softly through the car speakers. The lyrics felt like a whisper from the past, echoing the comforting words my beloved wife, Charlene, so often said: "Don't worry, honey, it will be alright." And with her by my side, it always was. Her steady presence grounded my world, giving me the strength to face whatever came our way.

But now, I'm not alright, and it's not all right. Maybe, if you've picked up this book, you're not all right either. Loss has a way of unraveling us, shaking the very foundations of who we are. It carves into our lives with the sharp sting of grief, leaving behind a hollow ache where love, joy, and connection once flourished.

I've been a priest for over 30 years and a chaplain for several police departments. I've taught seminars on meditation, spirituality, and stress management. I've counseled parishioners and police officers through their darkest hours—during their greatest losses and deepest heartbreaks. And yet, with all my experience and training, nothing could have prepared me for the tidal wave of grief I faced when my beautiful wife of 43 years was taken from me so suddenly.

We had plans to grow old together, holding on to each other until the end of time. Now, with her gone, I find myself repeating: I am only half a person, living half a life. She was my life, and without her, who am I? As George Harrison so poignantly sang, *"Tell me, who am I without you by my side?"*

Through this journey, I've come to understand that grief is as unique as the love we've lost. While spiritual and psychological practices can provide guidance, no one can truly know how *you* feel or what *you* are personally experiencing. Grief has become my constant, unwanted companion—one I've had to confront, accept, and even befriend. It is through this relationship with grief that I've learned to move forward, carrying the love that remains alive in my soul.

Grief isn't a condition to be cured or a challenge to overcome; it's a journey—a winding path we must walk. At times, it feels unbearable, like a weight pressing on our chest or the suffocating waves of endless tears. It's the gnawing realization that the life we cherished is forever changed.

Yet, even in the depths of pain, something endures love. It doesn't disappear with loss, though it transforms. The very existence of our grief testifies to the depth of the love we've known—a love so profound that its absence leaves us broken.

This book is not about "getting over" grief because I don't believe we ever truly do. Instead, it's a companion for those learning to live with it. It's for anyone searching for meaning amidst loss, striving to honor the love that remains while facing the emptiness that lingers.

Within these pages, I'll share my journey—moments of despair, glimpses of hope, and the ways in which love continues to speak, even in the silence. My hope is that through my story, you may find echoes of your own. Together, we can share the weight of this pain—a pain that, while heavy, also reminds us of the beauty of the love we've known.

Grief may never leave us entirely, but it reveals something profound: the love we carry is eternal. It transcends time, distance, and even death. This book is a testament to that enduring love—a love that will never die.

"But know this: When I have finished all of my days, it is my most sacred intention to find you again." – Alan D. Wolfelt

Prelude
Love, Life, and Loss: A Search for Answers in Grief

I remember the day as if it were etched into my soul. It was May 9, 2024, just over a week after my wife Charlene had been admitted to the hospital due to complications from stage 3 uterine cancer. Her oncologist had just delivered devastating news: the chemotherapy wasn't working, and she would now be coming home under hospice care.

When I arrived upstairs to see her, I greeted her with our usual joke: "Hoke is here to pick up Miss Daisy." It had become a tradition whenever I drove her to treatment. She would smile and say, "Thank you, Hoke." I'd reply, "No problem, Miss Daisy. Just text me when you're done, and I'll pick you up."

But that day felt different. As the physicians and nurses prepared her for discharge, we talked for what felt like hours. Finally, Charlene looked at me and said, "I don't want to do this anymore." I took her hand and replied, "But you know what that means, honey?" She nodded, and we both cried. I held her tightly until the nurse arrived with the discharge instructions.

A few days later, as I stood at the kitchen sink washing dishes, Charlene approached me. She seemed so small and fragile, wearing a chemo cap to cover her hair loss. Her voice was weak, and when she spoke, I looked at her with wide eyes as she asked a question that would forever be etched in my heart:

"So tell me, what was the purpose of all of this?"

At first, I thought she was asking about the treatments, but then it hit me—she was asking about life itself. Our life. The life we had built together. Turning to her, I said, "Char, look at all you've done, all we've done together. Our family would never be what it is without you. The faith you had in us and the love you gave us made us who we are.

"The purpose, honey, was love. The love we shared, the life we built together, and everything we created from that love. It's all about love."

She smiled at me, nodded, and quietly returned to her recliner. In the days that followed, we shared several deep conversations, though her strength was fading and words became fewer. On May 22, at 2:43 p.m., I watched Charlene take her last breath. At that moment, I knew I had lost the most essential part of my life.

Months have passed since Charlene's death, though it feels like centuries. Without exaggeration, we had a storybook life, a love Jane Austen would have written about. Charlene was the kind of person who lit up every room she entered, offering warmth and wisdom to anyone who crossed her path. Our children once said, "We never heard you and Mom yell or argue." I would always smile and respond, "What was there to argue about? Your mother was always right."

It wasn't that I was compliant in all ways. Oh, we had our disagreements. But we had a way of making decisions together, trusting each other's insight and intuition. Charlene was the heart of our family—our anchor, our guide, and my greatest love.

Still, Charlene's question haunts me: "So tell me, what was the purpose of all of this?" That question has inspired me to write this book—not only in memory of my loving wife but because I feel compelled to answer her.

Though deeply spiritual, Charlene carried baggage from her Roman Catholic upbringing. Over the years, she shed the idea of a judgmental God, but that lingering Catholic guilt remained. While she wasn't particularly vocal about my more mystical Christian beliefs—reincarnation, past lives, near-death experiences, or dream interpretation—she was always quietly listening. I believe she found solace in the idea that our journey together transcended this lifetime. When Charlene asked me her unforgettable question, she wasn't challenging my beliefs. She wanted to hear my answer.

A friend asked me about my next book over lunch some time ago. I told her, "I think I am done writing." She smiled knowingly and said, "You still have one more in you." In meditation, I heard Charlene's voice again: "So tell me, what was the purpose of all of this?" Moreover, I felt her nudge—to grieve and keep moving forward. Now, I feel she is urging me to explore this question in my final book.

This book is my attempt to answer Charlene's question. It explores love, life, and the meaning we can create even in the face of profound loss. It's a journey of grieving, celebrating the beauty of what we had, and finding purpose in what remains. Through these pages, I hope to honor Charlene's memory, share the comfort in our story, and offer support to others who are facing similar struggles. Ultimately, I hope to find my own way forward—and perhaps even, eventually, back to her.

So here I am, answering her question, hoping to help you—and myself—find meaning. Together, let's reflect on the purpose of this extraordinary life and how love endures, even beyond the boundaries of this world.

Part One - Purpose In Relationships

"The body is only a garment. How many times you have changed your clothing in this life, yet because of this, you would not say that you have changed? Similarly, when you give up this bodily dress at death, you do not change. You are just the same, an immortal soul, a child of God."
—Paramahansa Yogananda

Chapter One

Eternal Life—Death Is Not The End

From as early as I can remember, one belief has anchored me: the reality of eternal life. Death? I wasn't entirely sure what it meant or where it led, but deep within me was an unwavering conviction—my soul belongs to God. In that belonging lies eternal safety, a trust that God would never let my soul slip into nothingness.

In my previous book, *Finding God in the Extraordinary*, I described the soul as a flame lit by the Creator—a flame that, though it might flicker, can never be extinguished. The soul is eternal because it is of God, and what is of God does not perish. This understanding has shaped how I view life, death, and the purpose of our time here on Earth.

The soul is not merely an abstract idea; it is the essence of who we are—a spark of the divine. As I reflect on my wife Charlene's profound question—*"What was the purpose of all this?"*—I feel drawn to revisit this belief. Understanding the soul's eternal nature is key to finding meaning in life and death and embracing the truth that there is more life in death than in this one lifetime.

Let me begin with a story.

Years ago, Charlene and I sat together on our porch one quiet evening, the setting sun painting the sky with golden hues. It was a time we often shared—deep discussions over a glass of wine as the world softened in the twilight. That evening was no different. We talked about life, death, and the possibility of an afterlife.

I shared my belief in reincarnation—the soul's journey through lifetimes and its ultimate desire to reunite with its Creator. Charlene listened intently, though her expression revealed a hint of skepticism.

"So, what do you think happens after we die?" I finally asked her.

"To be honest? Nothing," she replied.

Her answer startled me. "What do you mean by nothing?"

She paused before explaining her belief in a void—a state of limbo where nothing happens. She admitted that this stemmed from her Roman Catholic upbringing, which had instilled a dualistic view of life: one earthly existence followed by judgment. It was a rigid framework that left little room for exploration or imagination.

Over time, as we continued these conversations, Charlene's perspective began to soften. While she didn't fully embrace my views, she entertained the idea of something beyond the "nothingness" she feared. "It's still a little too complicated for me," she'd say with a smile, but I could sense her openness growing.

Her honesty about her fear of the unknown deepened my determination to explore these questions—not just for myself but for her too. This book is part of that exploration, an attempt to shed light on the soul's progression and its ultimate reunion with the Creator.

The Journey of the Soul

Ancient traditions and spiritual teachings describe the soul as originating from the Creator's love. It is not merely energy or consciousness but a spark of the divine, existing beyond time and space. The soul is the eternal thread that connects our individual lives to a greater purpose—learning, experiencing, and sharing love.

In each lifetime, the soul gathers experiences, learns lessons, and sheds the layers of separation that obscure its true nature. This journey is one of remembering—remembering its divine origin and its connection to the Creator.

During one of my meditations, I envisioned my soul as a wave in a vast ocean, moving alongside countless others, all traveling toward the same distant shore. Each wave carried the essence of God's infinite presence, flowing forward with the hope of shaping a landscape filled with joy, peace, and love. This vision stays vivid in my mind, a reminder that the soul is constantly evolving, always seeking to manifest the divine.

The Three Loves of the Soul

I have seen love as the common thread that weaves through all of existence. The soul, as a reflection of divine love, is meant to experience and express this love in three essential ways:

Loving the Creator

Loving the Creator is not a duty; it is a natural yearning of the soul to reconnect with its Source. This love is nurtured through prayer, meditation, and moments of quiet reflection. After Charlene's passing, I had a profound meditation in which I felt her presence so clearly it was as if she were sitting beside me.

In that moment, I understood that love does not end—it transforms, transcending the boundaries of time and space. Love is with and within the creator.

Loving Ourselves and Others

Self-love and love for others are deeply intertwined. Charlene embodied this truth. Her quiet confidence and boundless compassion touched everyone she met. She taught me that honoring the divine spark within ourselves enables us to extend that love outward, forging meaningful connections with others.

Loving Creation

To love creation is to honor the sacredness of all things. Charlene's garden was a living testament to this truth. Each flower she tended seemed to reflect her belief in the beauty of life, even in its fleeting nature. She often said, "God is in the details," and her garden became a mirror of her spirit—a place of renewal, beauty, and divine connection.

Reflection

As I reflect on my beliefs about eternal life, I invite you to pause and consider your own.

- What do you believe happens after death? Is it a continuation, a transformation, or something else entirely? Perhaps you have had moments that made you wonder about the soul's eternal nature—a vivid dream, a sense of connection with a loved one who has passed, or a feeling of déjà vu that hinted at something beyond this lifetime.

- Take a moment to explore these questions in meditation or contemplation. Imagine your soul as a flame—flickering yet enduring. Where does that flame lead you? What does it reveal about the eternal nature of your being?

Meditative Thought

Love is the eternal thread that weaves meaning into our lives and our deaths. It is the origin and purpose of existence, the guiding star on the soul's journey. In this chapter, I hope to have shared a glimpse of the soul's eternal nature and its divine purpose. As we continue this journey together, may we uncover more of the love that binds us—to each other, to creation, and to the Creator.

"Love is patient, love is kind. It does not envy, it does not boast, it is not proud. It does not dishonor others, it is not self-seeking, it is not easily angered, it keeps no record of wrongs. Love does not delight in evil but rejoices with the truth. It always protects, always trusts, always hopes, always perseveres. Love never fails. And now these three remain: faith, hope, and love. But the greatest of these is love." — 1 Corinthians 13

Chapter Two
The Foundation of Love

A Declaration of Love

"I would love to come over and see you," I said, my heart pounding as I held the phone tightly.

Charlene's voice came back with a mixture of warmth and practicality. "You can, but I must study tonight for an exam, so I'll need to focus. If you come, bring a book to keep yourself busy."

I didn't hesitate. Though she lived in Woburn, north of Boston, and I in Quincy, south of the city, the hour-long trip through evening traffic seemed inconsequential. Something weighed heavily on my chest—a truth I needed to tell her, one I couldn't bring myself to say over the phone.

We had been dating for some time, and I knew I was deeply in love with this extraordinary woman. It felt as though my life had been a prelude to meeting her. Yet I hesitated, unsure if she felt the same. The drive to Woburn was a cocktail of excitement and anxiety. I rehearsed what I would say over and over: Charlene, I love you. Then doubt crept in: What if she doesn't feel the same?

When I arrived, Charlene greeted me at the door with a kiss. "You'll have to sit over there and not bother me while I study," she teased, pointing to a chair across the room.

I settled in with a book, though I couldn't focus on a single word. My eyes kept drifting to her. The light from the desk lamp highlighted her auburn hair, and the way she tucked a strand behind her ear as she concentrated made my heart ache with affection. Occasionally, she glanced up and smiled a simple yet profound gesture. Each time, I thought, *Say it now!* But what if…

After an hour of this internal debate, I couldn't hold it in any longer. "Charlene?" I called softly.

She looked up. "Yes?"

"Come sit on my lap. Just for a moment."

She raised an eyebrow, her playful skepticism evident. "I thought I told you to stay over there?"

"Just for a moment," I urged.

Finally, she relented, crossing the room and settling into my lap. Her arm wrapped around my neck, and her eyes met mine. "Well?" she said with a mischievous smile.

"Look at me," I said, my voice trembling.

"I am," she replied, her tone softening.

"No, really. Look into my eyes."

Her expression shifted from playful to curious. I took a deep breath. "Charlene, I love you. I am in love with you."

The seconds stretched into what felt like an eternity. Then, her lips curved into a smile that lit up her entire face. "I love you too," she said, yet with a depth that took my breath away.

At that moment, the foundation of our life together was laid. The love we declared for one another that night would grow and endure, becoming a guiding force through every joy and challenge to come. Even now, though she is gone, that love remains unchanged and unbroken.

The Nature of Love

As Saint Paul wrote, "The greatest of these is love." But what does that truly mean? Is love merely a feeling, fleeting and ephemeral, or is it something far more profound, far greater?

In the early days of my relationship with Charlene, I saw love as a gift—a rare and precious treasure to be cherished. But over time, I understood that love is also a teacher. It shapes us, challenges us, and, if we allow it, transforms us.

Love taught me patience. I was never the most patient man. Charlene often teased me about my tendency to rush through life but never lost her temper. Instead, she gently reminded me that life unfolds in its own time. Once, during a particularly stressful period at work, I came home frustrated and short-tempered. Charlene simply listened, her calm presence diffusing my tension. "Take a breath," she said. "This too shall pass." Her ability to ground me in the present moment was a testament to her quiet strength and the patience she brought into our relationship.

Love also taught me vulnerability. That night in Woburn, when I told Charlene I loved her, I was taking a risk. My heart was laid bare, and the possibility of rejection loomed large. Yet, in that moment of vulnerability, I discovered the strength of love. By daring to share my deepest self, I created a connection that transcended fear and doubt.

Most importantly, love taught me about purpose. Through our shared dreams and quiet moments, I came to see that love is not just something we experience—it is something we give. It is how we show up for one another, how we forgive, and how we build a life together.

Lessons of Love

One winter, during a snow blizzard, we found ourselves snowed in. Charlene was thrilled and suggested we make the best of it. Of course, Charlene spent the day cooking, and then we ended up playing board games and dreaming about our future. That evening, as the snow continued to fall, we cuddled, wrapped in blankets. "This is life, and today, we just made a hard day better," she said softly.

That simple statement stayed with me. Love, I realized, is not just about grand gestures or dramatic moments. It's about everyday acts of kindness and understanding, about the way we create warmth and light for each other, even in life's storms.

Eternal Love

Even now, with Charlene gone, her love remains. It is in the lessons she taught me, the memories we created, and the way she shaped who I am. Her question, "What is the purpose of all of this?" lingers in my mind. The answer, I believe, is love, our love. Love is eternal. It is the thread that connects us to each other and to something far greater than ourselves. As Saint Paul wrote, "Love never fails." And in its enduring nature, love reminds us of our own eternity.

Reflection

As you read this, I invite you to reflect on your own journey with love:

- Who has taught you the most about love? Was it a parent, a partner, a child, or a friend? What did their love reveal to you?

- When has love felt most alive in your life? Was it during a joyful celebration, a quiet moment, or even a time of loss? What did that teach you about love's depth?

- How do you give and receive love? In what ways do your actions, words, and presence convey love to those around you?

- Lastly, consider the love you show yourself. Do you offer yourself the same grace and compassion you extend to others? Loving yourself is not selfish; it is the foundation from which all other love flows.

Love has a way of leaving its imprint on our souls, guiding us toward our higher purpose. It connects us, teaches us, and challenges us to grow. As you reflect, may you discover how love has shaped your journey and what it continues to teach you about life's greater meaning.

"*The greatest legacy anyone can leave behind is to positively impact the lives of others.*" – Emeasoba George

Chapter Three
Family As Legacy

A New Beginning On May 1, 1981, Charlene and I began our life together as husband and wife. We were deeply in love, but as the years passed, we faced an unspoken ache: the dream of having children eluded us. By our tenth anniversary, despite our best efforts and prayers, we had come to accept the possibility that parenthood might not be part of our journey. Yet, life has a way of surprising us when we least expect it. At the latter part of 1991, we received news that felt like a miracle: we were going to have a baby.

Our Quiet Garden of Hope

Christopher's arrival on January 22, 1992, transformed us in ways we could never have imagined. His birth marked the beginning of a new chapter, one filled with laughter, sleepless nights, and a love that expanded with each passing day. Before long, our family grew to include Caroline, Emma, and Timothy. Our once-quiet home became a vibrant symphony of giggles, footsteps, and endless questions. Our love had now grown into something larger than ourselves. It wasn't just about the bond between two people anymore—it was the foundation of a family, a living legacy built on shared values and unwavering commitment.

Before Christopher's arrival, Charlene's backyard garden was a quiet refuge, and I was her "go-for." I watched as she poured her hopes into the soil, planting flowers and vegetables as if each seed held a whispered prayer. We'd sit on our deck on summer evenings, watching the sun dip below the horizon. In those moments, we learned to find peace in waiting, to see beauty in what was growing, even when the deepest longings of our hearts went unanswered. The gardens she nurtured taught us patience, faith, and the art of nurturing—not just plants but each other.

Years later, as we watched our children play in a yard surrounded by Charlene's masterpieces, we realized how those lessons in the garden had quietly prepared us for the joys and challenges of parenthood. Our home became more than just a place to live; it became a sanctuary where love was cultivated, and lessons were learned. In the simple rhythms of daily life—meals around the dining table, bedtime stories, and impromptu kitchen baking parties—we discovered the essence of family. These moments formed the foundation of a legacy that would extend far beyond the walls of our home.

The Nature of Family

Charlene had a remarkable way of balancing her roles as wife, mother, and teacher. She didn't just care for our children; she empowered them. Through her example, they learned the importance of kindness, honesty, and perseverance. She taught them to embrace challenges and celebrate victories, no matter how small. I often marveled at her ability to see the potential in each of our children. While I might have focused on solving problems or providing, Charlene looked deeper, nurturing their individual gifts and dreams, like a gardener tending to each plant. Her love was not only tender but transformative, shaping the people they would become.

Lessons in Legacy, Parenthood.

I've come to realize it is not about perfection. It's about presence. It's about showing up, even when you're tired, and listening, even when the world is noisy. It's about teaching values through actions, not just words.

One summer evening, as the sun set behind our backyard garden, Charlene and I watched the children play, laughing and having fun. She turned to me and said, "Who would ever think? Harry. We were planting a garden a few years ago, and today, we're planting seeds for a future we may never fully see."

Her words have stayed with me, a reminder of the profound responsibility and joy of parenthood. Every bedtime story, every moment of patience, and every shared laugh was a seed planted in the soil of their hearts. These seeds, we hoped, would grow into a legacy of love, resilience, and faith.

The Gift of Memories

Memories are the threads that weave together in a family's story. We all treasured our vacations on White Horse Beach, where the ocean's waves seemed to echo our children's laughter. I remember the joy-filled chaos of Christmas mornings, the scent of Charlene's homemade cookies filling the air as the kids tore into their presents. These moments were more than fleeting joys; they were the foundation of our children's understanding of love and togetherness. Even the challenging times became part of our story. When life threw us curveballs, we faced them together, drawing on each other for strength from the bonds we had forged. Through every high and low, our family remained a testament to the power of love and faith.

Charlene and I understood that our legacy was not in material wealth but in the values we instilled. Faith in God, the importance of integrity, and the value of hard work—these were the principles we sought to embody and pass on. We often spoke of these truths, but more importantly, we lived them.

Our actions became lessons in themselves. The way we treated others, approached challenges and loved each other spoke volumes. We hoped these values would guide our children long after we were gone.

Eternal Family

Charlene's question—"What is the purpose of all of this?"—has taken on new meaning for me as I look back over the years in memory. Part of the answer lies in the family we built. It is in the love we shared, the values we upheld, and the memories we created. But it also lies in something greater: the recognition that our family was a co-creation with our Creator, God.

Through the joys and challenges, we were stewards of God's love, entrusted with the sacred task of shaping lives and nurturing souls. Our family became a reflection of His divine plan, a space where patience, forgiveness, and grace flourished.

Ultimately, our legacy is rooted in love. It is the story we leave behind, written not in words but in the lives we touch. And in that story, I find peace, knowing that the love Charlene and I shared will continue to resonate through generations.

Reflection: Your Family, Your Legacy

As you consider our family's story, I invite you to reflect on your own. What seeds are you planting in the lives of your loved ones? Are there traditions you cherish, values you uphold, or memories you strive to create?

Could you take a moment to think about the legacy you wish to leave behind? If your family were a garden, what would you hope to see flourishing in the years to come?

Reflect on the small, everyday moments that might seem insignificant now but will one day become cherished memories. Consider the lessons you teach, not just through your words but actions. And remember, it is never too late to plant seeds of love, kindness, and faith.

Your family's legacy is not just about the past but about shaping the future. Each act of love and grace becomes a thread in the tapestry of your story, a story that will endure long after you are gone. Let that story be one of faith, hope, and, above all, love.

"How do we change the world? One random act of kindness at a time. Kindness is a gateway for all of us to connect and care for each other." —Morgan Freeman

Chapter Four
The Impact of Friendship and Community and the Rippling Effects of Kindness

A Lesson in Kindness

"May I have a medium hot coffee, cream, and two Equals?" I asked the drive-thru speaker.

"A medium black with two Equals," came a snippy reply.

"No. A medium hot coffee, cream, and two Equals."

"A medium with cream?" The response grew sharper, more impatient.

Frustration bubbled up inside me, threatening to boil over. "My Lord!" I snapped, letting my irritation spill into my words. "A medium hot coffee with cream and two Equals!"

Charlene, ever my calm anchor, touched my arm gently. "Now, now, Honey, why be so nasty? The poor girl might be having a horrible morning."

"She might be having a horrible morning, but that's no reason to make mine just as bad," I retorted.

Charlene didn't argue. She said softly, "Just be nice."

When we pulled to the window, a frazzled young girl handed me my coffee. "I am so sorry, sir," she said, her voice sincere and sweet. My frustration melted instantly, replaced by a wave of embarrassment.

Charlene turned to me with a knowing smile. "See? Just be nice."

That simple phrase became one of the many lessons Charlene taught me during our 44 years together. Although patience may not have been my strongest suit, Charlene's gentle persistence reminded me that kindness could transform any situation. Her wisdom lingered long after the moment had passed, teaching me that compassion—even in the smallest exchanges—has the power to shift perspectives and lighten burdens.

The Power of Lifelong Friendship

Charlene's kindness wasn't confined to her family; it radiated outward, touching friends, neighbors, and strangers alike. One of the most profound examples of her capacity for friendship was her relationship with her cousin Nancy.

Nancy was not just family; she was Charlene's confidant, her cheerleader, her unwavering rock. A year older and more outspoken, Nancy balanced Charlene's quieter, gentler nature. Together, they were inseparable—"besties" long before the term became popular.

Charlene often said that the song, *Wind Beneath My Wings* reminded her of Nancy because, in their younger years, it was Nancy who lifted her, gave her strength, and encouraged her to soar. Their bond was a testament to the friendship that becomes part of your very being—a friendship that shapes your soul.

One day early in our relationship, I got a glimpse of just how much Charlene valued Nancy's opinion. We had taken a day trip to Sturbridge Village in Massachusetts, and Charlene invited Nancy along. Over lunch, Charlene excused herself, leaving Nancy and me alone at the table.

Nancy leaned in, her tone serious. "Harry, may I ask you something?"

"Of course," I replied, a bit curious.

"Have you ever been married?"

Her question caught me so off guard I nearly fell out of my chair. "What? No! Where would you even get that idea?"

Nancy explained that someone had told Charlene's mother I was divorced with two children. It didn't take long for us to unravel the confusion—it was my brother they'd been referring to, not me.

Nancy burst into laughter, just as Charlene returned. Without missing a beat, Nancy said, "That's his brother, not him." Charlene's look of relief was unmistakable. When I asked later why she hadn't asked me directly, she admitted she'd been afraid I might think she didn't trust me.

That moment, though funny in retrospect, revealed the depth of Charlene and Nancy's relationship. Nancy wasn't just a cousin; she was Charlene's sounding board, her partner in navigating life's uncertainties. Their friendship was a beacon of loyalty and love, illuminating the value of having someone who knows you deeply and supports you unconditionally.

When Nancy passed away suddenly at 62, Charlene was heartbroken. "I've lost my best friend," she said through tears. But even in her grief, Charlene honored their bond by carrying Nancy's memory forward. She became the kind of steadfast friend Nancy had always been to her, offering others the same love and support she had received.

The Ripples of Connection

Through Charlene, I saw how friendships—whether they last a lifetime or bloom briefly—become part of who we are. They shape us, lift us when we're low, and challenge us to grow. Charlene created ripples of kindness in her relationships that spread far beyond what she could see.

Each interaction she had, no matter how small, was a chance to plant a seed of kindness. Charlene understood that these seemingly minor acts could create waves of positivity, whether it was a simple smile to a stranger, a warm hug for a friend in need, or a heartfelt note of encouragement. She taught us that even the briefest connections hold the power to transform a day, a moment, or even a life.

One winter, when a dear friend of hers traveled to Florida, Charlene knew the property needed looking after. Despite the fierce wind and heavy snow blanketing the roads, she insisted we make the journey to secure the house.

I wasn't thrilled. The weather was dreadful, and I complained the whole way there, my frustration rising as the snow piled up around us. But Charlene remained calm and focused on the task at hand. After a long, exhausting drive, we arrived at her friend's house, and she set to work, making sure everything was in order.

Once the work was done, we drove to the nearest restaurant and sat down for a leisurely lunch, the storm outside now nothing more than a backdrop to the warmth inside. Charlene smiled at me and asked, "See, now, was that as bad as you thought?"

I couldn't help but laugh, realizing she had been right all along. What had seemed like an impossible, frustrating task had turned into a peaceful moment—a reminder of her quiet strength and unwavering care for those she loved.

Friendship and Community as Reflections of Divine Love

Friendship and community are among life's greatest gifts. They remind us that we are not alone—that we are part of something larger. When we nurture these connections, we create spaces where people feel valued, understood, and loved. The bonds we form, whether fleeting or enduring, act as threads weaving the fabric of a compassionate and supportive community.

Kindness has a power all its own. A simple gesture—a kind word, a patient smile—can spark a chain reaction, inspiring others to carry that kindness forward. Like a pebble dropped into still water, each act of compassion creates ripples that touch countless lives. These ripples often extend beyond what we can see, influencing others in ways we may never fully understand.

True friendship is rooted in love, trust, and mutual respect. It mirrors the divine love that flows from the Creator—unconditional, enduring, and ever-expanding. In friendship, we catch glimpses of God's grace.

Community, too, reflects this divine love. It is where we learn to care for one another, to bear each other's burdens, and to celebrate each other's joys. When we open our hearts to others, we allow the light of the Creator to shine through us, making the world a kinder, more compassionate place. Isn't this, ultimately, the purpose of our journey? To leave behind ripples of love that will endure long after we are gone.

Reflection: Your Friendships, Your Community, Your Ripples

Take a moment to reflect on the friendships that have shaped your life. Who has been your "Nancy"—the person who has lifted you when you needed it most? Have you been that person for someone else?

Think about the ripples you're creating in your community. How are your words and actions impacting those around you? What kind of legacy are you building through your relationships?

Charlene's simple reminder to "just be nice" was not just a suggestion but an invitation to live with intention. It taught us that even the most minor acts of kindness carry the power to change the world.

As you move through life, consider the ripples you leave behind. No matter how small, each act of love becomes part of a larger story—a story of connection, compassion, and divine love.

Part Two - Purpose In Challenges

"There will always be trials and tribulations in life, but God will carry you through every storm in your life and give you strength to make it" (Ephesians 3:20).

Chapter Five
Trials and Tribulations

She woke up in the middle of an October night, clutching her abdomen and whispering, "I am in a lot of pain. I think I had better go to the hospital." Her voice, usually calm and steady, now wavered with urgency. Charlene never complained—not once in the 43 years we had been married. She was a nurse, stoic by nature, and always focused on others. If she said she needed the emergency room, I knew the pain must be unbearable.

The hospital was just up the street, but that short drive felt like an eternity. I held her hand tightly as we made our way inside. They took her in for tests and scans while I sat in the waiting room, staring at the clock. When she returned, I stood up immediately.

"What did they say?" I asked, trying to steady my voice.

Charlene, always composed, began to cry. The sight of her tears broke something in me.

"I think I am in trouble," she said softly.

I wrapped my arms around her and held her close. "What do you mean?"

She took a deep breath and replied, "They found a mass on my uterus. They want me to see an oncologist."

Her words hung in the air like a heavy cloud. We sat in silence for a moment, letting the weight of them settle. Finally, I said, "We will get through this, honey. Together."

In my heart, I believed it. We had faced so many challenges over the years, always emerging stronger. I clung to the hope that this time would be no different.

The diagnosis came quickly: stage 3C uterine cancer. It was rare, aggressive, and the tumor was too large to remove surgically. The doctors recommended chemotherapy to shrink it before attempting surgery.

Charlene approached the treatments with remarkable bravery. The first sessions brought minimal side effects, and she always managed to smile through them. One evening, as she noticed the first strands of her hair falling out, she stood in front of the mirror, gently running her fingers over her scalp. Then she turned to me with a wry smile and said, "Well, I guess I won't need a hairbrush anymore."

But the second round of chemotherapy hit her harder. Her appetite faded, and she grew thinner and weaker. One morning, as I watched her quietly sorting through her closet, I asked, "Why are you doing that?"

She looked at me with eyes full of understanding and said softly, "You're in denial."

"I'm not in denial," I insisted. "I'm just holding out hope."

She gave me a sad smile. "Sometimes hope looks different than we expect."

After the second round, the cancer spread to her pancreas. The doctors suggested more chemotherapy, combined with injections. By then, Charlene was so frail that I had to carry her to the car for appointments. Each trip to the hospital became more agonizing.

On one such day, they admitted her directly to the hospital ward. It was our 43rd wedding anniversary. I stayed by her side, holding her hand as the hours stretched into days. After a week, she was discharged into hospice care. She came home on May 9.

On May 22, at 2:43 in the afternoon, Charlene took her final breath. I was by her side, holding her hand, as the best part of me slipped away. Not once during her illness did she complain. She faced every moment with grace, kindness, and even humor. Her strength left me in awe.

In the following months, I spent countless hours reflecting on her journey. Charlene's unwavering courage taught me that challenges are not just obstacles to overcome but opportunities to grow. Through her pain, she showed me what it means to live fully—even in the face of death.

Her illness forced me to confront questions I had long avoided: What is the purpose of suffering? How do we find meaning in pain? Charlene's quiet strength became my guide. She taught me that the purpose of challenges is not always to conquer them but to meet them with love, dignity, and faith. Her journey revealed a profound truth: challenges refine us, deepen our capacity to love, and bring us closer to understanding the eternal nature of the soul.

Reflection: Your Challenges

As I walked through this journey with Charlene, I wondered: What role do challenges play in our lives? How do we respond when faced with hardships, and what do those responses reveal about us?

I invite you to pause for a moment and ask yourself:

- How do you react when faced with a challenge? Do you approach it with strength and faith, or do fear and doubt paralyze you?

- What have your struggles taught you about yourself? Have they revealed parts of your character that you did not know existed? Have they shown you a depth of resilience or compassion you did not expect?

- In the face of suffering, how do you find meaning or purpose? Is it in the love and support of those around you? Is it through spiritual reflection or perhaps a deeper understanding of your own soul?

- Do you believe that challenges have a purpose beyond the pain? Can you look back at past struggles and see how they shaped you into who you are today?

In my experience, Charlene's illness brought me face-to-face with these questions. While I did not always have the answers, I learned that part of the journey through challenges is asking these questions and being open to the answers, no matter how they come. As you reflect on your challenges, I encourage you to look for deeper meaning in the struggles you have faced. What have they taught you about love, resilience, and the very nature of your soul?

"We do not have to rely on memories to recapture the spirit of those we have loved and lost – they live within our souls in some perfect sanctuary which even death cannot destroy." — Nan Witcomb

Chapter Six
Loss and Grief as Teachers

On September 25, just four months after losing my beloved wife, Charlene, my 15-year-old Cockerpoo, Cooper, took a turn for the worse and passed away. They say losing a devoted pet is like losing a child, and I found this to be profoundly true. My heart shattered once again, and I reached the lowest emotional ebb of my life.

Cooper had been my constant companion, my shadow, and my source of joy for all those years. Mischievous and filled with life, he embodied unconditional love in its purest form. I have always believed that our pets never live as long as we wish, but just long enough to inspire within us the boundless love God intended for humanity to experience. Perhaps that is why "dog" has the same three letters as "God"—a reminder of the divine, unconditional love that fills our hearts, souls, and minds.

Suddenly, a home that, only a year ago, had been alive with Charlene's laughter, her playful banter, and the soft pitter-patter of Cooper's paws became unbearably silent. It felt as though the house itself grieved, its emptiness echoing the void in my soul. My heart and spirit were only half present; I felt like half a man in half a world, living only half a life.

Charlene had been my life and world; Cooper was my closest and most loyal companion besides her. His passing plunged me into what many call the "Dark Night of the Soul." Though I was surrounded by love, I felt adrift and profoundly alone. If there was a lesson to be learned from this overwhelming grief, it remained hidden, shrouded in the depths of my sorrow.

Amid this overwhelming sorrow, I began to reminisce about the deep conversations Charlene and I had before her passing. I remember asking her tearfully, "What will I do without you?" She had replied, "Live. Live for the children." For Charlene, the children were the most important part of our legacy—the greatest treasure we left behind.

I also told her how wonderful our life had been, how much we had accomplished, and how deeply we had loved. She smiled and said, "Just like Kenny Rogers' song, 'Through the Years.'"

Yet, despite these comforting memories, the grief was overwhelming. It cut through me like a knife, and I often broke down over the simplest things. My constant companion now became my sorrow. I knew I could never get back what I once had, and I understood that the pain would always be with me.

Finding Light in Darkness

Gradually, I began finding ways to cope. I started attending Saturday evening church services, which brought a sense of peace. Meditation became a lifeline, helping me center myself. I set aside time to write and play my piano and guitar, allowing music to soothe my aching soul. I even went out for lunch with friends, trying to stay busy despite the ever-present grief.

In moments of stillness—through dreams and meditation—I could feel Charlene's presence. Her love and spirit inspired me to keep moving forward. Grief became my teacher, pushing me to grow and honor Charlene's wish: "Live."

Moving forward was anything but straightforward. Grief often felt like an unpredictable tide, pulling me under when I least expected it. Certain memories surfaced without warning: the comforting way Cooper would curl up beside me in the evenings or the warmth of Charlene's laughter filling the room during her favorite movies. These recollections were both a balm and a sting—a bittersweet reminder of the life we once shared.

One afternoon, as I sifted through old photo albums, I found myself immersed in the stories each page told: family vacations, birthdays, and quiet moments at home. Every image seemed to hold its own voice, drawing me back to those cherished times. Grief, I realized, had its own way of preserving these memories, allowing me to relive them with striking clarity. In those moments, it felt as though Charlene and Cooper were gently reaching across time to remind me of the joy we had shared. Their physical absence was undeniable, but their essence remained alive, woven into the fabric of my being.

Grief, the Teacher

Grief is a companion none of us wish to meet, yet it arrives unbidden and draws us into its transformative embrace. At first, I felt as though grief was a weight too heavy to bear—a relentless storm that swept through my life, dismantling all that was familiar. Yet within this storm was an invitation to learn, grow, and live.

I am slowly learning that loss strips us of our illusions of permanence and reminds us that nothing in this world is truly ours to keep—only ours to love, cherish, and eventually release. In the depths of this surrender, we are taught the fragility of existence and its profound beauty. What would love mean if it weren't intertwined with the inevitability of loss?

For me, the losses of my beloved Charlene and my faithful Cooper were more than mere events; they were lessons inscribed on my soul. I am learning to try to look past the pain and into the heart of what these losses reveal. Through grief, I have rediscovered my capacity to love deeply, to hold memories as sacred, to treasure those closest to me, and to be kind to everyone.

Through prayer and meditation, I often ask the Creator to help me understand the purpose of my pain. Slowly, I am beginning to see that grief is not just about what is taken away but also about what it leaves behind. It has deepened my empathy for others and strengthened my appreciation for the fleeting moments of joy life offers. Each sunrise feels like a gift, and each interaction with a loved one is a treasure.

In its wisdom, grief is not only about what we lose but also about what we gain—a deeper understanding of ourselves, a renewed connection to others, and, sometimes, an awakening to the divine presence that sustains us. When we allow grief to teach us, we are drawn closer to the Creator, finding a sacred thread that weaves loss and love together into the tapestry of our lives and allows us, once again, to live.

Reflection: Embracing Loss and Grief as Teachers

Grief often feels like an unwelcome visitor, but its lessons, though painful, can shape us in profound ways. As I navigated my losses, I discovered truths about love, impermanence, and the enduring connection to those we hold dear.

Now, I invite you to take a moment to reflect on your own journey:

- Have you experienced a loss that changed how you view love or life?

- In moments of grief, what helped you keep going or find meaning?

- How do you honor the memory of those you have lost?

- Do you believe there is a lesson hidden in grief? If so, what might it be?

Write your thoughts down or meditate on them. Reflecting on your feelings can help you uncover the more profound wisdom loss and grief offer.

Part Three - Purpose Beyond The Self

"No act of kindness, no matter how small, is ever wasted." – Aesop

Chapter Seven
Service to Others

A winter storm was barreling toward us, and I sat listening to the weather forecast, trying to assess what preparations were needed. Just as the meteorologist announced the storm's anticipated severity, a loud rat-a-tat-tat erupted from Charlene's sewing room. The familiar sound made me smile.

It was that time of year—the church Christmas Fair was just around the corner, and Charlene was in her element. The upstairs was a whirlwind of activity: fabric swatches scattered like confetti, patterns draped over chairs, and her sewing machine humming tirelessly as she crafted pillows, quilts, blankets, and aprons. Her meticulous dedication transformed our bedroom into a showroom of completed projects, each imbued with love.

Downstairs was no less alive. The kitchen was thick with the aroma of her famous red pepper relish simmering on the stove—a fair favorite that never lasted long on the tables. Soon, the oven would be working overtime to bake Mimi cookies, a cherished recipe that Charlene brought to life every year. Her contributions were not merely items for sale—they were pieces of herself, given freely and joyfully, ensuring the fair's success year after year.

Charlene's selflessness extended far beyond these fairs. One winter, she braved icy roads to check on a friend's Cape Cod home while they were away in Florida. She did it without hesitation and without expectation of thanks—that was simply who she was. Her giving spirit often manifested in quiet acts of care, unnoticed by many but deeply felt by those on the receiving end.

I remember one particularly busy Christmas season when her aging sewing machine began to act up. The thread kept tangling, the needle stuck, and yet Charlene persevered. "Why don't you just get a new one?" I asked, watching her frustration grow.

She shook her head, her voice gentle but firm. "Oh, I can't do that. Christmas is coming, and there are too many other things we need."

Charlene's reluctance wasn't rooted in frugality for its own sake; she was always thinking of others. Later that evening, I noticed her browsing sewing machines online. She lingered on a Husqvarna Viking model, her eyes lighting up for a moment before she sighed and closed the page.

That Christmas, I surprised her with the very machine she had hesitated to buy for herself. Her reaction was unforgettable—a mixture of shock, joy, and overwhelming gratitude. For someone who gave so much and asked for so little, it felt like the smallest way to honor her immeasurable kindness.

Charlene had a profound understanding of purpose. To her, it wasn't about grand gestures or accolades. It was found in the simple, quiet ways she poured love into the world—through her actions, her talents, and her unwavering care for others.

Her career as a nurse exemplified this truth. She tended to Veterans with a compassion that extended beyond duty. Each patient received not just her medical expertise but her genuine humanity. She saw them not as numbers or cases but as people deserving of dignity and care.

Her sewing, too, was an extension of her love. She stitched warmth and thoughtfulness into every project—an apron for a friend, a quilt for a newborn, costumes for church plays. These were more than objects; they were tokens of her heart, each thread connecting her to the recipient.

And then there was her cooking. Charlene's kitchen was a sanctuary of love and hospitality. Whether she was delivering a casserole to a grieving family or baking treats for a community event, her food carried an unspoken message: *You are cared for. You are not alone.*

Her garden was yet another reflection of her giving spirit. Charlene transformed our yard into a living tapestry of vibrant flowers and greenery. It wasn't just for her enjoyment; it was a gift to the neighborhood. Passersby often stopped to admire her handiwork, drawn to the beauty she had cultivated.

But perhaps what I admired most was the *how* of her giving. Charlene approached every act of kindness with humility and joy. She sought no recognition, only the quiet satisfaction of knowing she had brightened someone's day.

Through her life, Charlene taught me—and so many others—that service is not a duty but a privilege. It is in the giving of ourselves that we discover our true purpose. Her legacy is a testament to the power of kindness, proving that even the smallest acts can create ripples that touch countless lives.

Reflection: Your Service to Others

As I reflect on Charlene's life, I am struck by how deeply she understood the transformative power of service. She showed me that purpose isn't found in seeking fulfillment for ourselves but in giving of ourselves to others.

- So I ask you: How do you serve? In what small, quiet ways do you bring light to the lives of those around you?

  Perhaps it's a kind word to a stranger, a meal shared with a friend, or a talent you use to create something meaningful. Whatever it may be, recognize its significance. Each act of service, no matter how small, contributes to a greater tapestry of love and connection.

- As you ponder these questions, consider this: Service is not just something we do for others; it is a way of aligning ourselves with a purpose greater than our own. In giving, we find meaning. In serving, we find ourselves.

"Yes, pray often for those who have passed on. This is part of your consciousness. It is well. For God is God of the living. Those who have passed through God's other door often listen for the voice of those they have loved in the earth." – Edgar Cayce

Chapter Eight:
Spiritual Reflections

Prayer, Meditation, and Dreams as Dialogue with the Divine

In Finding God in the Extraordinary, I explored prayer, meditation, and dreams as profound means of connection—one that transcends simple verbal requests or expressions of gratitude. As I see them, prayer, meditation, and dreams are not merely rituals but pathways to transcendent consciousness, a union with the Divine. They can shape our inner state and, perhaps, even our reality. These spiritual practices have always been part of my life and have opened the door to profound insights, spiritual growth, and experiences beyond ordinary perception.

For me, the most meaningful prayer is deeply personal, whether it takes the form of silent introspection or an outward conversation with God, spoken as if He were present before me—because, in my heart, I believe He is. Through meditation, I've learned to quiet my mind and open myself to deeper awareness. In that stillness, I find a connection to the underlying fabric of reality and to the Divine.

Dreams, too, hold a valuable place in our existence, offering a unique way for God and our loved ones to communicate with us through messages and symbols. These beliefs have shaped how I approach prayer, meditation, and dreams. Through this lens, I invite you to reflect on their roles in your life.

Rediscovering Spiritual Practices

During Charlene's illness and for a time after her passing, my prayer and meditation practice felt like a closed door. I had always turned to these spiritual elements as a source of solace and clarity, but in those first months, it became a struggle. My mind, weighed down by grief, would not settle. Even when I tried, the stillness I once found so quickly seemed unreachable.

Adding to the difficulty, my physician had prescribed medication to help me cope with the depression and loss. While it provided some relief from the rawness of my emotions, it dulled the connection I felt during prayer and meditation, making it harder to focus and harder still to listen. Eventually, I stopped the medication and decided to rely on the practices that had always been my guide.

One day, I sat in quiet determination, letting go of any expectations. I did not try to force stillness or clarity. With no goal but to sit in the moment, I allowed myself to be.

And then, everything shifted. It was as though a dam had broken, and the flow of connection I had been longing for returned. I could feel responses in my prayer—a sense of direction. In my meditation, I could see Charlene—not as a memory but as a presence. I felt her warmth, her love, and her gentle encouragement.

A Dialogue Beyond the Veil

In the days following Charlene's passing, I spoke to her as if she were still here. Sitting in her favorite chair or walking through the garden she loved, I would say her name aloud, share my thoughts, and ask the questions that lingered in my heart. It felt natural, as though the boundaries between this life and the next had softened.

One afternoon, while shopping at one of Charlene's favorite stores, HomeGoods, I reminisced about the last time we had been there together. Emotion welled inside me, and as tears threatened to fall, I quietly asked her: Charlene, what was the purpose of all this? Your illness, our love, the life we built together—what did it all mean? Can you hear me? Are you here with me?

There was no audible answer, but I felt her presence as surely as if she had placed her hand in mine. In my mind, her voice came through, clear and steady: "It was love. That is all it ever needed to be."

After composing myself and paying for the items, I walked to the car. As I approached the driver's side door, I noticed something on the ground—a brand-new cloth bracelet with the word Believe embroidered on it. It was as if Charlene had made it and left it there for me, a sign to reassure me.

That moment has stayed with me as a testament to the depth of our connection and the power of love to transcend even death. It was not just my imagination—the same Charlene who had comforted me through life's challenges was now guiding me from a place I couldn't see.

The Role of Dreams in Connection

Dreams became a vivid and profound way for Charlene to reach me. Initially, my dreams after her passing were fleeting and unclear, often filled with the fragmented emotions of grief. But as I deepened my meditation practice and began to pray with a quieted mind, the dreams shifted. They became vivid, purposeful, and filled with unmistakable symbolism.

In one dream, I saw Charlene in a radiant garden, vibrant with colors that seemed otherworldly. She looked as she had when we first met: youthful, with her flowing hair catching the light. She was smiling, her joy unmistakable. She didn't need to say much, but her presence spoke volumes. It was as if she was saying, "I'm fine, and I'll be here waiting."

This dream, and others like it, became an anchor for me. Each one felt like a gift—a reassurance that she was at peace and that our bond remained unbroken. Through these dreams, I came to understand that love is a bridge that even death cannot dismantle.

Reflection: Your Spiritual Experiences

- As I have shared my journey of prayer, meditation, and connection with Charlene, I find myself wondering about your own experiences. Have you ever considered how you connect with the divine, with loved ones who have passed, or even with your inner self?
- I invite you to take a moment of stillness and reflect: What practices bring you peace and a sense of connection? Do you feel the presence of your loved ones in subtle signs, dreams, or moments of deep clarity? Have you experienced the warmth of divine love in quiet prayer or felt guided by intuition in times of need?
- Allow these questions to guide your thoughts and, if you feel inspired, write down your reflections. This is a sacred opportunity to explore the ways you find meaning, comfort, and connection in your life. Embrace what comes to you, knowing that your spiritual journey is as unique and extraordinary as you are.

Chapter Nine
Conclusion: Finding the Answer

As I sit with Charlene's question—*"So tell me, what was the purpose for all of this?"*—I feel the weight and beauty of what she was truly asking. It wasn't just a question for me, but for life itself: for the cherished moments, the struggles, and everything in between. After much contemplation, I have come to realize that the answer lies in the simple yet profound truths of love, relationships, and legacy.

Love is the essence of life's purpose. It is the force that connects us, sustains us, and imbues every moment with meaning. Love is not always loud or grand. It is found in the quiet moments of devotion, the patience we show in hardship, and the willingness to put others' needs before our own. Charlene taught me that love is less about what we feel and more about what we give. She embodied this every day—in her compassion as a nurse, in how she cared for our family, and in the way she nurtured her garden as if it were a reflection of her soul.

Relationships give shape to this love. Through them, we are refined and strengthened. They teach us patience, humility, and forgiveness. Relationships test us, revealing both who we are and who we are meant to become. In loving Charlene, I learned that relationships are sacred because they are where love lives—alive, growing, and evolving as we do. Even after her passing, I feel our connection deepening, as if love transcends time and space, weaving its way into eternity.

Legacy is what remains after we are gone. It is the culmination of our love and relationships, the imprint we leave on the lives of others. Charlene's legacy is vivid and enduring. It lives in those she comforted, in the neighbors who marveled at her garden, and in the countless meals and pastries she lovingly prepared. It lives in me, in our children, and in everyone she touched. Legacy is not just what we leave behind; it's what we sow in the hearts of others, what we build together, and what endures in the lives we've shaped.

Laughter

Laughter was one of Charlene's most endearing traits. If her family had to describe her in a single word, it would undoubtedly be "love," but laughter was an inseparable second. Her laughter wasn't just a sound; it was an experience, a ripple of joy that swept everyone into its embrace. Whether in a quiet living room or a bustling gathering, when Charlene laughed, the room transformed. Her laughter would start as a gentle chuckle and then build into an irresistible wave of mirth, often leaving everyone in stitches without even knowing the cause.

There's a story that still warms my heart—a simple yet vivid moment that captures Charlene's infectious humor and the bond we shared. It was one of those ordinary evenings, and I was busy feeding the dogs. Charley, our spirited yellow lab who weighed about 55 pounds, bounded toward me in her excitement and landed squarely on my lightly covered foot. The pain shot through me like a hammer strike, and I let out a yelp, hopping around the room in what must have been a comical frenzy.

Instinctively, I glanced at Charlene, who was seated at the table. Her eyes sparkled with that unmistakable mix of artificial concern and amusement. "Are you all right?" she chuckled, her voice steady but her expression betraying her true emotions. Before I could reply, I noticed the subtle bounce of her shoulders—her valiant but doomed effort to stifle a laugh. The sight of her trying to hold it in was irresistible, and suddenly, the pain didn't matter anymore. We dissolved into laughter, the kind that bubbles up from somewhere deep inside and leaves you breathless.

Later, still smiling, Charlene confessed, "It wasn't just the situation. It was the way you hopped around—you were so dramatic!" This wasn't an isolated incident. Charlene had a knack for finding humor in life's little mishaps, especially mine. She teased me lovingly, her laughter never mocking but always a shared joy. It was as if she had a gift for transforming the mundane or even mildly frustrating moments into opportunities for connection and lightheartedness.

That was Charlene—her laughter wasn't just about humor; it was about connection. Laughter became our way of turning life's stumbles into shared memories, a reminder that even in pain, there's room for joy when you're with someone who truly sees you. Her laughter was more than just an expression of amusement; it was a language of love. It reminded me that even in life's imperfections—a mishap of silly, clumsy moments—there is beauty and humor to be found. Laughter, in its purest form, is a way of saying, "I'm here with you, in this moment, sharing this joy."

In the weeks and months after Charlene's passing, I found myself replaying those moments in my mind. Her laughter echoed in my heart, a comforting reminder of her spirit. One evening, as I sat in quiet reflection, I thought I heard her laugh—soft, distant, yet unmistakably hers. It was as if she was reminding me not to take life too seriously, to find humor even in the midst of grief.

Laughter is a universal language, a bridge that connects us to one another and to life itself. It transcends barriers, dissolves tensions, and invites us to be fully present. It's a precious gift Charlene gave to everyone she met, and one I strive to carry forward.

As you read this, I invite you to take a moment to reflect:

- Can you recall a time when laughter brought unexpected joy to a difficult moment? How did it shift the energy and bring people closer?

- Have you ever laughed so freely that it felt like a weight had lifted from your shoulders? What was it about that moment that made it so special?

- Does someone's laughter—perhaps from a loved one who has passed—still echo in your memories? How does it make you feel, and how does it shape your connection to them?

Consider journaling your thoughts or simply holding them in your heart. Laughter, after all, is a tribute to life's fleeting beauty. It reminds us that even in the midst of sorrow, there is always room for joy. As Charlene taught me, sometimes the most profound connections are found in the simplest, silliest, and most unexpected moments.

Believe

When Charlene asked, *"What was the purpose for all of this?"* I believe she already knew. Her life was a testament to the answer: to love fiercely, to connect deeply, and to leave the world better than we found it. Her question gifted me a compass—a way to navigate her loss and find my purpose moving forward.

I now believe that purpose is not something we find but something we create. It is written in the love we give, the relationships we nurture, and the legacy we leave. Charlene and I wrote that purpose together, line by line, day by day. And though she is no longer here, our story continues.

A Closing Vignette

While driving down the road one day, speaking aloud to Charlene as I often do, I was suddenly struck by a profound sense that my surroundings were only temporary. It felt as though I was partially present in another, more beautiful, and unearthly space. Everything around me appeared sharper, more vivid, and more alive. I sensed that Charlene was sharing a glimpse of her new reality with me, gently saying, *"It is so different, so beautiful; it is another dimension of existence. And I will be here for you."*

A few days before this experience, I had been drawn to Neal Donald Walsch's book *Conversations with God*. Walsch writes that God speaks to us through our thoughts, feelings, and experiences. I found myself reflecting deeply on the word "experience." Was it only past experiences or something more?

One morning, just before sunrise, I felt Charlene's presence again while meditating in bed. It was as though she were softly telling me that God is present in every experience we've ever had. God speaks to us, showing us the way, while allowing us the freedom to choose our path. Later, I felt these thoughts wash over me:

Our spiritual journey is like breathing. Each breath we take is a gift from God, just as our free will is. We can choose to hold our breath, resisting the flow of God's Spirit, just as we sometimes resist His guidance in life. This is a choice we often make, even though God leads and sustains us. But just as we cannot hold our breath forever, we cannot resist God's Spirit indefinitely. At some point, we must breathe again, allowing the life-giving flow of His presence to sustain us. We come to understand that the truest way to live is not by holding our spiritual breath but by allowing God's Spirit to guide and infuse every experience.

In every moment, God is there. In every experience, God is speaking.

Chapter Ten
Sixteen Exercises to Help Cope with Grief

Grief is a deeply personal journey, and finding practices that resonate with your soul can offer comfort and healing. Below are exercises to help you navigate this path:

1. Meeting Grief Head-On

How to Practice:

- Allow yourself to sit with your grief without distractions. Begin by sitting comfortably or lying down, allowing yourself to become fully present. Close your eyes if it feels natural, and take a few deep breaths to ground yourself. Acknowledge your feelings fully, whether through quiet reflection, speaking aloud, or journaling. Avoid the temptation to "keep busy" as a way to divert your attention. Remember, meeting grief head-on aligns with embracing and processing emotions rather than avoiding or suppressing them. This approach allows individuals to confront their pain, work through it, and ultimately integrate the experience into their lives.

- You might want to name your emotions aloud or in your mind: "I feel sadness," "I feel anger," or "I feel lost."

- Consider journaling about your thoughts and emotions as they come. Write without censorship, allowing your grief to flow onto the page freely.

- If you prefer speaking, you can talk to a loved one, a therapist, or even aloud to yourself or your departed loved one. Express what is on your mind or heart as if they are listening.

Avoid distractions like scrolling through your phone, watching TV, or diving into work. Instead, focus on being with your emotions. If the feelings become overwhelming, use grounding techniques such as deep breathing, holding onto a comforting object, or touching the ground to center yourself.

Why It Helps:

Grief is an intense, multifaceted emotion that demands acknowledgment. Confronting grief directly fosters emotional processing and helps integrate the experience into one's life, leading to more profound healing and understanding. Avoidance can prolong or intensify grief, while facing it helps one recognize its depth, honor its presence, and gradually integrate it into one's life story. This practice also deepens self-awareness and builds emotional resilience.

2. Nature Walks

How to Practice:

- Choose a natural setting that resonates with you—a local park, a hiking trail, a beach, or even a quiet garden. If you're unable to leave your home, sitting near an open window or tending to indoor plants can offer a similar sense of connection.

- Leave behind your phone or set it to silent to reduce distractions. Begin walking slowly and intentionally, focusing on each step. Feel the texture of the ground beneath your feet, the air on your skin, and the rhythm of your breathing.

- Use your senses fully: notice the details of your surroundings, like the way sunlight filters through leaves, the sound of wind, or the scent of flowers.

- Pause occasionally to stand still and absorb the energy of the moment. Breathe deeply and let nature's beauty fill your senses.

- If your mind starts to wander, gently guide your attention back to your surroundings.

- If it feels natural, speak aloud to your loved one, your Creator, or yourself. Share your thoughts or ask for guidance, letting nature serve as a silent witness.

- Consider carrying a small notebook to jot down any insights, emotions, or observations that arise during your walk.

Why It Helps:

Nature Walks reconnect us with the rhythms of life and provide a sense of grounding. Walking in a natural setting reduces stress, calms the nervous system, and fosters mindfulness. Nature's beauty and tranquility remind us that life continues to flow, offering us comfort and renewal even in the midst of grief. It also allows for moments of contemplation and connection with our loved ones in spirit as we become more receptive to subtle signs and messages.

3. Meditation

How to Practice:

- Find a quiet, comfortable space where you won't be disturbed. Sit or lie down in a relaxed position and close your eyes. Take a few deep breaths, allowing your body to settle.

- Begin by focusing on your breath. Feel the natural rhythm of your inhalations and exhalations, letting your mind rest on this simple anchor.

- If you're using tools like HemiSync, let the sounds guide you gently into a state of relaxation.

- Visualize a warm, radiant light surrounding you. This light represents love, peace, and healing. Imagine it filling you, warming and soothing every part of your being.

- If it feels right, visualize your loved one surrounded by the same light, sending their love and reassurance to you. Picture them smiling or offering comfort, creating a space where you feel their presence.

- Allow your thoughts to flow naturally, observing them without judgment. If your mind wanders, gently bring your focus back to your breath or visualization.

- Close your practice with a moment of gratitude or a brief reflection on how you feel.

Why It Helps:

Meditation helps quiet the mind and bring peace to an otherwise restless heart. It allows us to sit with our emotions without judgment, creating space for healing. Through visualization and focused breathing, meditation fosters a sense of presence, making it easier to process grief in a healthy way. It also opens the door to spiritual connections, offering glimpses of love and reassurance from those we have lost.

4. Prayer

How to Practice:

- Approach prayer as an intimate conversation with your Creator. Sit or kneel in a peaceful space, and speak openly, as if the divine presence is right before you.

- Share your joys, grief, hopes, questions, and gratitude. Let your words flow naturally, expressing whatever is on your heart.

- After you've spoken, take a moment of silence to listen. Trust that answers, guidance, or comfort will come in the way you need, even if it isn't immediate.

- If you prefer, write your prayers in a journal. This allows you to reflect on them over time and recognize patterns of growth or insight.

- Create a ritual around your prayer practice: light a candle, hold a meaningful object, or sit in a designated prayer space to deepen your connection.

- Consider incorporating sacred texts, affirmations, or meditative music if they resonate with you.

Why It Helps:

Prayer provides comfort by offering a direct line of communication with the divine. It gives us a space to express our emotions, from sorrow and longing to gratitude and hope. By speaking openly and listening in stillness, we cultivate faith that we are supported and guided. Prayer reminds us that we are not alone in our grief and that love endures beyond the physical realm.

5. Dreams

How to Practice:

- Before bed, set an intention to connect with your loved one or receive insight through your dreams. You might say aloud or silently, "I invite a message, a sign, or comfort in my dreams tonight."

- Create a calming bedtime routine to prepare your mind for intuitive dreaming. This might include dimming the lights, listening to soft music, or engaging in gentle meditation.

- Keep a dream journal or notebook by your bed. The moment you wake, write down everything you remember from your dreams, even if it's just fragments, emotions, or symbols.

- Reflect on your dream entries, noting any recurring themes, symbols, or feelings. Over time, you may discover patterns or messages that resonate deeply.
- If you feel inspired, use the insights from your dreams in your creative expression or meditation practice.

Why It Helps:

Dreams offer a bridge between the conscious and subconscious mind, often bringing comfort and insight. They can serve as a medium for reconnecting with loved ones, receiving guidance, or processing emotions that are difficult to face during waking hours. Recording and reflecting on dreams can help uncover hidden emotions, patterns, or messages that bring peace and healing in the grieving process.

6. Laughter (Charlene's Favorite)

How to Practice:

Dedicate time to activities or memories that bring joy and lightness to your heart. Watch a favorite comedy show or movie that you and your loved one enjoyed together. Read a humorous book, listen to stand-up comedy, or revisit funny anecdotes or inside jokes you shared with your loved one.

- You could also create a "laughter journal" where you jot down funny memories or moments that made you laugh during the day.

- Explore laughter yoga, a practice that combines intentional laughter exercises with deep breathing to enhance physical and emotional well-being.

- Share a laugh with friends or family by playing games or recalling joyful memories during gatherings.

Why It Helps:

Laughter isn't just a distraction from grief; it's a powerful tool for healing. It releases endorphins, relieves stress, and provides moments of lightness that remind you of the love and joy your loved one brought into your life.

7. Journaling

How to Practice:

Set a consistent time each day to sit with your journal in a quiet, reflective space. Begin by writing whatever comes to mind—your emotions, thoughts, or questions you may have for your loved one. You might structure your journaling in different ways, such as:

- Writing a letter to your loved one, sharing your day or expressing what you miss most about them.

- Capturing a cherished memory in detail to preserve it.

- Exploring your feelings and observations about your healing journey.

- Reflecting on insights or messages that come to you during meditation, prayer, or dreams.

Consider using prompts like:

- "Today, I felt close to you when..."
- "What I wish I could tell you..."
- "A memory that brought me comfort today..."

Why It Helps:

Journaling offers a safe space for exploring your emotions without judgment. It fosters self-discovery, emotional release, and a deeper connection to your loved one's memory. Over time, your entries can serve as a map of your healing journey.

8. Creative Expression

How to Practice:

Identify a creative activity that resonates with you. This could be painting, drawing, sculpting, composing music, or writing poetry. Let your emotions guide your creative process.

- Create a piece of art or music inspired by your loved one, incorporating symbols, colors, or melodies that remind you of them.
- Use a blank canvas to express your feelings visually, even if abstractly.
- Write a story or poem that celebrates your loved one's life or captures your experience of grief and healing.

If you're not sure where to start, try setting an intention like, "I'll create something that expresses my love and gratitude."

Why It Helps:

Creative expression transforms intangible emotions into tangible forms, offering a channel for catharsis and a way to honor your loved one. It can bring clarity and meaning to your journey.

9. Gratitude Practice

How to Practice:

At the close of each day, reflect on the moments that brought gratitude to your heart. Write down three things you're thankful for, no matter how small. These might include:

- A memory of your loved one that surfaced during the day.
- Acts of kindness you experienced or witnessed.
- Simple joys, like a beautiful sunset or a comforting cup of tea.

You might also dedicate one of your entries to your loved one, expressing gratitude for their influence on your life and the memories you shared.

Why It Helps:

Focusing on gratitude shifts your attention from loss to abundance, highlighting the enduring presence of love and kindness in your life. It cultivates resilience and an appreciation for the beauty that surrounds you.

10. Breathwork

How to Practice:

Find a comfortable, quiet place to sit or lie down. Practice a rhythmic breathing pattern such as:

- Inhaling deeply through your nose for a count of four.
- Holding your breath gently for a count of four.
- Exhaling slowly through your mouth for a count of six or eight.

As you breathe, visualize releasing tension with each exhale and inviting peace with each inhale. Placing a hand on your chest or belly can help you stay connected to your breath.

You might also explore guided breathwork sessions or apps for deeper relaxation.

Why It Helps:

Breathwork not only calms your body and mind but also grounds you in the present moment, creating space for healing and clarity amidst emotional turbulence.

11. Connection with Others

How to Practice:

Reach out to someone you trust and share your feelings openly, knowing that vulnerability is a strength. You can:

- Join a grief support group where others can relate to your experience.

- Schedule regular check-ins with family or friends to share stories about your loved one.

- Allow yourself to both give and receive support, fostering mutual healing.

If speaking feels difficult, consider sharing your thoughts through written messages or emails.

Why It Helps:

Human connection reminds you that you are not alone. Sharing stories, receiving empathy, and supporting others lightens the emotional load and nurtures a sense of community.

12. Rituals of Remembrance

How to Practice:

Create meaningful rituals to honor your loved one, such as:

- Lighting a candle at the same time each evening while reflecting on a cherished memory.

- Planting a tree or tending a garden in their memory, watching it grow as a symbol of their enduring presence.

- Creating a memory box with photos, letters, and mementos that you can revisit when you wish to feel close to them.

- Preparing a meal or engaging in an activity they loved on significant dates.

Why It Helps:

Rituals provide a structure for remembering your loved one and nurturing an ongoing connection. They bring comfort and a sense of continuity, allowing you to honor their legacy.

13. Mindful Movement

How to Practice:

Engage in gentle, intentional movement practices such as yoga, tai chi, or stretching. Focus on the sensation of your body as you move, syncing your breath with each motion.

- Choose poses or movements that feel soothing, such as child's pose or a gentle sway.
- Use movement as an opportunity to release physical tension and invite emotional release.

Walking meditation is another mindful practice: take slow, deliberate steps while focusing on your surroundings or breath.

Why It Helps:

Mindful movement reconnects you with your body and the present moment, fostering emotional balance and physical relaxation.

14. Service to Others

How to Practice:

Look for ways to give back that feel meaningful to you and honor your loved one's values. This could include:

- Volunteering at a charity or organization they cared about.
- Helping a neighbor or community member in need.
- Making a donation in their name to a cause they supported.

Small acts, like writing a kind note or offering a listening ear, can also make a big difference.

Why It Helps:

Serving others channels your energy into meaningful action, creating a sense of purpose and connection. It also brings healing by spreading kindness and love in your loved one's memory.

15. Reading and Reflection

How to Practice:

Choose books, poetry, or spiritual texts that resonate with your grief and healing journey. As you read, take time to reflect on passages that speak to you, jotting down your thoughts or how they relate to your experience.

- Consider reading aloud, as the spoken word can deepen your connection to the text.

- Engage in discussions with others or join a book club focused on themes of loss and resilience.

Why It Helps:

Reading provides wisdom, comfort, and a sense of solidarity through shared experiences. It encourages introspection and offers new ways to navigate your journey.

16. Visualization

How to Practice:

Sit in a quiet space, close your eyes, and imagine yourself surrounded by a warm, radiant light. This light represents love, comfort, and peace.

- Visualize your loved one smiling at you, their presence filling you with reassurance and warmth.
- Picture the light expanding, enveloping you and your surroundings, creating a cocoon of peace.

Spend several minutes in this state, letting the visualization wash over you before gently returning to the present.

Why It Helps:

Visualization nurtures a deep sense of calm and connection. It reminds you that love transcends physical boundaries, offering solace and peace in moments of grief.

Each exercise is an invitation to honor your grief, celebrate your love, and find moments of healing along the way. You can choose the practices that resonate with you and return to them as needed. Healing is not linear, but with time and intention, you can rediscover peace and purpose in your life.

A Final Word of Encouragement

As you approach the final page of this story, I want to leave you with a message of encouragement. Life's purpose is not distant or hidden—it is waiting to be embraced in the moments we live each day. It is in the love we give, the relationships we nurture, and the legacy we create through our choices and actions.

I invite you to reflect on your own journey: on the people who have shaped you, the passions that ignite your spirit, and the ways you can leave the world better for having been here. Purpose does not require perfection. It thrives in our imperfections, in the courage to keep growing, giving, and loving despite life's challenges.

Remember, purpose is not something we stumble upon by chance. It is something we cultivate through mindfulness and intention. It is found in how we treat others, the dreams we pursue, and the gratitude we hold for life's extraordinary gifts. Even in times of loss or uncertainty, purpose remains a guiding light, reminding us that every life has value and every moment has meaning.

So, go forth with an open heart and a willingness to seek the extraordinary in the ordinary. Cherish the people you hold dear. Love deeply and unconditionally. And know that by doing so, you are creating a legacy that will endure far beyond your time here.

Life's purpose is yours: to discover, shape, and share. May you find it, live it, and cherish it every step of the way, just as Charlene and I did during our 43 blessed years of marriage.

Thank you. Charlene and Harry.

www.ingramcontent.com/pod-product-compliance
Lightning Source LLC
LaVergne TN
LVHW010557070526
838199LV00063BA/4997